CW00520560

Wakeboarding Basics: All About Wakeboarding

ISBN-13: 978-1479291069
ISBN-10: 1479291064

Copyright Notice

WAKEBOARDING BASICS: ALL ABOUT WAKEBOARDING

Kim Roughton

I dedicate this to the lucky few who've been touched by the joy, excitement and buzz of wakeboarding...

Contents

Wakeboarding:
An Introduction

Wakeboarding is said to be the sport of the times.

It involves balancing on a wakeboard and then being towed behind a boat at speeds of around 18-24mph.

The sport is similar to waterskiing, but uses a single board, which is wider and shorter than a snowboard and comes with foot bindings.

Surfing used to be the beach lover's favourite sport for many years, but in 1985, a hybrid of the surfboard and the waterski was invented by a surfer named Tony Finn and given the name Skurfboard.

The new board looked like a small surfboard and the rider rode it while being pulled by a boat and performing some new skills and tricks.

Foot straps were later added to the board, which allowed riders to perform even more dynamic stunts. That sport was referred to as Skurfing at that time.

Soon after that, a successful waterskiing businessman refined the boards to enable riders to perform even more stunts and in doing so, completely changed the sport.

Other sports companies soon followed suit and the sport finally gained a wider audience in 1992, when a Florida-based sports and events promoter started organising wakeboarding events.

The events gave wakeboarders the opportunity to compete at professional levels while gaining exposure on international sports stations at the same time.

And when World Publications launched Wakeboard Magazine in 1993, the sport gained even more validation on a global scale.

As each year passed thereafter, support for both the magazine and the Pro Wakeboard Tour continued to grow.

As proof of this continued support, various wakeboard cups have been launched over the years and these competitions are widely attended and eagerly awaited by wakeboard enthusiasts worldwide.

For an average beach dweller, the pull of wakeboarding is quite obvious.

It's generally much easier to learn than surfing and you typically feel a lot safer, since you have something to hold on to.

In fact, the fact that there are handles that serve as support is considered a real perk by many people.

Aside from these, wakeboarding offers a lot of other advantages.

For one thing, you can engage in the sport anytime you want.

Unlike surfers who need to follow the waves, you can engage in wakeboarding on any beach and at any time of the day as long as you have a good boat to pull you along.

Wakeboarding also provides you with a lot of opportunity for self-expression.

The sport gives you the freedom to strive for greater heights when you perform your stunts.

Today, there are more than three million people who actively participate in the sport of wakeboarding all over the world.

In fact, the sport has gained such popularity that a video game about it was created and released in 2003.

Wakeboarding has also become part of Gravity Games and the X-Games, thus attracting more attention and gaining more credibility as one of the extreme water sports.

Right now, about 75% of wakeboarding participants are male, but the number of female participants is slowly making a dent on this currently male-dominated sport.

Wakeboarding is, in fact, today's fastest-growing water sport.

Learning about Wakeboarding

Wakeboarding, a surface water sport, uses the combined techniques of surfing, waterskiing, and snowboarding.

In this sport, the rider is balanced on a wakeboard and then tagged behind a speeding boat.

As he rides the wake, the rider also performs a number of tricks. The speed of a wakeboard boat depends largely on factors such as the size of the wakeboard, the water conditions, the rider's weight, and the rider's preferred speed.

Wakeboards look like a cross between a surfboard and a water ski, but they're slightly curved for an easier lift. Wakeboard bindings help riders keep their feet on the board.

A wakeboarder typically wears a wetsuit and either moves towards the wake or drifts away from it in order to perform different tricks.

To perform jumps, for example, you'll have to hit the wake and then leap into the air. You may also choose to use the slide bar and ride the wake while keeping your balance.

Once you've mastered riding the wake and jumping, you can start learning to execute tricks while you're in the air.

If you want to increase your speed as you approach a wake, all you need to do is tighten your wakeboard rope.

Take note as well that a tightened rope effectively helps you launch into the air and then perform your aerial tricks.

The size and shape of a wakeboard can vary according to your body weight and personal preference. Take note that the bigger the wakeboard is, the better it floats and edges.

However, bigger boards can make it more difficult for you to successfully execute some advanced stunts.

Your stunts may also be affected by your wakeboard's rocker or camber. Rockers, in particular, favour a faster and smoother ride without any surface resistance. Rockers and cambers also favour more aerial tricks into the wake.

Take note as well that most wakeboards are designed with fins, which are typically found at the bottom of your wakeboard.

The fins help you obtain more stability and make steering a lot easier, which make them very useful to beginners in the sport.

Just like any other freestyle sport, you'll need to practice a lot in order to master the various tricks and techniques in wakeboarding.

The good thing is that wakeboarding allows you to perform a wide variety of tricks once you get the hang of it.

One important thing you need to remember is that you're likely to perform much better wakeboarding tricks if you're able to attain more height.

Aerial grabs, in particular, are best executed at a good height, which makes you appear as if you're drifting through the air.

This trick is where you clutch the tow rope in one hand and then grab your wakeboard with the other.

Of course, there are also plenty of wakeboarding stunts you can perform without having to launch yourself into the air.

These tricks include the backside start, backside butterslide, potato peeler, bodyslide, and surf curve, among others.

These and the other techniques and tricks in wakeboarding have indeed made this wet 'n wild sport truly exciting!

Why You Should Try Wakeboarding

As summer approaches, families often find more time to bind with each other and enjoy some fun activities together.

Summer generally just means more quality time and more fun for many people.

And of course, summer will never be complete without people going to the beach and enjoying some of the most popular water sports.

One particular type of water sport that has recently caught the interest of both the young and old is wakeboarding.

Although this sport has just recently earned worldwide popularity and recognition, it has actually been around for a number of decades already.

One of the main reasons why many people aren't aware of the sport is that it's actually a sort of combination of a few popular water sports like waterskiing and surfing.

In fact, wakeboarding has so many similarities to surfing that it was once called skurfing before it was finally recognized as an entirely different sport and renamed wakeboarding.

Nevertheless, the sport of wakeboarding still makes use of the basic principles that are also being used in surfing and waterskiing.

If you've ever seen someone riding a board and holding onto a rope while being pulled along by a motorboat, then you already have an idea what wakeboarding is.

And if you think that's exciting, then you should see what participants in competitive wakeboarding can do!

Competitions are a lot more exciting because it involves greater speeds and more spectacular stunts.

Wakeboarding has indeed come a long way since it was first invented and it is now ranked among the world's most popular competitive sports.

In fact, a wakeboarding association has already been established and the sport is now included in the X Games.

If you're interested in getting into the sport, then you'll have to arm yourself with a good wakeboard, a motorboat, and a rope.

Of course, you don't really have to buy a motorboat of your own; you just need to gain access to one.

The good news is that there are plenty of wakeboarding areas that provide motorboats for rent and there are also lots of wakeboarding enthusiasts who are willing to share their motorboats with their peers.

The fact that you're being pulled along by a very fast-moving boat with only a rope as support certainly makes wakeboarding so much more exciting than many other water sports.

What makes it even more fun is that it allows you to practice and execute a lot of different stunts such as the Whirlybird, Elephant, and Tantrum.

These are perhaps the main reasons why more and more people are becoming interested in getting into the sport.

Add to that the fact that there are lots of wonderful places all over the world that offer excellent wakeboarding opportunities and you'll surely understand why this has become one of the most popular sports in the world.

If you're an adventurous woman, then you'll surely appreciate the fact that wakeboarding is also becoming more and more popular among women these days.

Even competitive wakeboarding has already been invaded by a lot of women.

But, just like any other sport, you'll have to master the basic wakeboarding skills before you even think about practicing any of the more complicated wakeboarding stunts.

Choosing Your Equipment

If wakeboarding has caught your interest, then you're likely to want to give the sport a try.

Among the most important things you need to consider before getting into this extreme sport is getting the right equipment for it.

Remember that getting the right equipment is the necessary first step towards ensuring safety in wakeboarding.

Bear in mind that wakeboarding is classified as an extreme sport, which means that it involves a significant amount of danger.

Take note as well that a majority of wakeboarding accidents occur because of defective equipment.

This is why you need to make sure all of the equipment you use is of good quality, from your wetsuit to your boots and your wakeboard bindings.

Safety should be of utmost concern when you get into this sport.

In order to choose the right wakeboarding equipment, you'll have to know exactly what you should be looking for.

The basic pieces of equipment required in the sport are the wakeboard, bindings, skates, handles, pylon, fins, boots, and helmets.

It's important to take your skill level into consideration when choosing the right wakeboard.

Wakeboards with square edges are usually recommended to beginners because they allow you to control the board easily.

Bigger wakeboards are also recommended for beginners because they generally offer more stability.

Aside from your skill level, it's also important to choose a board that suits your wakeboarding style.

If you're a beginner, then you may also want to ask a more experienced friend to assist you in choosing your board.

Fibreglass wakeboards are considered as the most durable boards and can serve their purpose for several years.

Boards made from this material can even withstand harsh weather conditions and isn't likely to get distorted the way boards made from other materials do.

Perhaps the only drawback is that fibreglass can be relatively expensive. But, if can afford a fibreglass wakeboard and if you plan to take up the sport professionally, then that may indeed be the perfect choice for you.

The durability and longevity of the board could very well be worth its price.

Once you've found the perfect wakeboard, you should make sure the bindings and boots you get fit the board perfectly as well.

This is why it's very important for you to check all three pieces of equipment very carefully before making an actual purchase.

The measurements of all three should fit perfectly with each other.

Of all the necessary wakeboarding equipment, the bindings are perhaps the most critical, since they help you keep your feet on the board while you perform wakeboarding stunts.

This makes it even more important for you to thoroughly check the bindings before buying them.

Among the most effective ways to ensure you're getting the right wakeboarding equipment is to buy it from a reputable store.

Do a bit of research to learn where wakeboarding professionals get their stuff so you can be assured that you're getting equipment of only the best quality.

You may also want to ask your friends who've been participating in the sport for some time for advice as regards the right equipment.

Above all, you should make sure the equipment you choose are durable and comfortable so you can always give the game your best shot.

Quick Guide to Choosing Wakeboarding Rope

If you've developed a fondness for wakeboarding and want to get into the sport professionally, then you need to realise how important the wakeboard rope is.

It is, after all, the only thing that connects you to the motorboat when you go wakeboarding.

This sport can indeed be a fun activity, whether you're doing it for competitive or purely recreational purposes.

The young and old alike can enjoy wakeboarding as long as they have the necessary balancing skills to ride the waves and glide through the air.

Of course, you'll have to learn the basics first and one of the most important things you need to learn is how to handle the wakeboard rope.

A wakeboard rope can vary in length from a minimum of 60 feet, most wakeboard ropes measure about 70 feet.

Some wakeboard ropes also feature length adjustments.

These ropes also come in a variety of elasticity and you can choose the degree of elasticity according to your personal preference.

Take note, however, that tighter ropes enable you to perform wakeboarding tricks and air stunts much easier.

And if you're a beginner in this sport, then a shorter wakeboard rope may also be much more practical and useful, as it allows you to stay closer to the motorboat.

You can fix a wakeboard rope onto the motorboat itself or mount it on a wakeboard tower, which generally provides more stability and gives you leverage as you perform your air stunts.

A tower can cost anywhere from a minimum of a thousand dollars, depending primarily on the quality and the brand.

Wakeboarding requires very little in terms of basic equipment because all you'll really need are the wakeboard, a motorboat, and a wakeboard rope.

However, there are several accessories you can use to spice up your game and add excitement to the sport.

You can choose to attach some lights to a wakeboard tower as well as a pair of speakers to make the game even more fun.

Wakeboarding is generally participated in by beach lovers during the daytime, but there are also those who prefer enjoying the sport at night.

If you're one of these people, then wakeboard tower lights will definitely be very useful.

Even if you have good tower lights, though, and you can see the area well enough, you should still make sure you're wearing the proper head gear so as to protect yourself from serious injuries.

Wakeboarding may seem quite harmless as you watch professionals glide through the air and perform various air tricks.

Take note, however, that the sport has been included in the X Games not only for the excitement it offers, but also for the level of danger associated with the sport.

You should therefore be cautious at all times and always consider your safety first, whether you're wakeboarding for fun or to compete.

Above all, you need to remember that wakeboarding isn't just a matter of balancing yourself on the wakeboard while holding on to a rope tied to the motorboat.

If you really want to master wakeboarding, then you'll also have to learn how to keep yourself afloat while lying on your back in the water.

Wakeboarding isn't as easy as you may think and you'll have to be a very good swimmer as well as a patient leaner in order to master it.

Wakeboarding Guide
for Beginners

If you're new to wakeboarding, then you'll definitely need the following guide on how to get started.

Most beginners in this sport have common questions and the guide will provide you with the answers to those questions.

Once you get these answers, you should be able to get out on the water and start riding the waves in no time at all!

What type of wakeboard should you buy?

The wakeboard you choose should suit your skill level as well as the boarding style you plan to do.

Wakeboards are designed with different features and other variables such as the size and shape of the board will determine the way it will perform as well. You may want to ask an experienced friend for advice on how each type of board works.

What shape should you choose for your wakeboard?

Beginners are generally advised to choose a wakeboard with squared edges.

This is because they provide more stability and control, which make it ideal for someone who isn't quite ready for the big tricks and air stunts just yet.

Once you've mastered the basics and are ready to go to the next level, you can switch to a wakeboard with rounded edges, which make it easier to land after performing air stunts.

This design also makes you less likely to catch and edge when you land and provides the board with more lift and speed when you jump.

Wakeboards also have either a single-tip or double-tip design. Single-tip boards are squared off at one end and pointed at the other, whereas double-tip boards are generally rounded at both ends.

The rounded ends allow easy transition when you switch directions and land after each trick. Most of the boards currently being sold are double-tipped.

Double-tip boards are also advisable for beginners because it allows you to perform the basic movements more easily.

Most of the double-tipped boards are also much lighter and easier for you to jump with.

How long should your wakeboard be?

The length of a wakeboard can vary according to its manufacturer. A single wakeboard model typically comes in two or three different lengths.

In general, however, wakeboards for smaller individuals range from 125cm to 135cm. For medium-sized individuals, the advisable length is from 135cm to 140cm and for large individuals, the ideal length is from 140cm to 145cm.

Beginners are often advised to go for longer boards because they offer more stability.

What else is there to know?

Once you've chosen the right wakeboard, you need to take a couple more things into consideration before actually hitting the water.

Most boards come with its own set of fins, but if yours don't, then you'll have to buy ones that suit your board and riding style.

Make sure the fins are secured tightly, with its wider end towards the outside of the board.

Take note that longer fins track more easily in the water and generally makes you feel more stable.

On the other hand, shorter fins will release more easily from the water.

Beginners are advised to choose longer fins, especially if they're wakeboarding in choppy waters.

Wakeboarding Basics

The reason why more and more people are now getting into wakeboarding is that it gives you an adrenaline rush that's just too exhilarating for most to resist.

As you probably already know, having the right wakeboarding equipment is important to mastering this sport, but having the desire and commitment to learn is just as essential.

Take note, however, that having the right equipment doesn't mean getting a pro board even when you're just starting out in the sport.

In fact, a larger wakeboard fitted with bigger fins may be the best board for a beginner because it allows you to manoeuvre the board more easily to whichever direction you want.

Learning how to point the board towards the right direction is, in fact, one of the most important steps in learning how to wakeboard.

Another important consideration when learning how to wakeboard is the length of your wakeboard rope.

A shorter rope is often recommended for beginners because it allows you to move closer to the boat.

Remember to start slowly, since you'll need just a bit of speed when you're just starting out.

As the wakeboard is just beginning to move, you can expect to feel a bit more resistance and you shouldn't forget to let the boat driver know that you want to start slow.

Next, you'll have to learn where and how to position yourself on the board. In doing so, it's necessary to identify your lead foot.

Ask someone to push you from the back and then observe which foot you instinctively step forward with to catch your balance; that is your lead foot.

Whichever your lead foot is, you need to position it in front of your other foot when you step onto the wakeboard.

Most people use the right foot as the lead foot, while only a few lead with the left foot.

This is why a right lead is called normal whereas a left lead is called a goofy lead.

Bindings are also among the most important considerations when learning to wakeboard.

As a beginner, you'd do well to place your bindings at shoulder width and position your rear foot near the back fin for better stability when you change directions.

The angle of your bindings is also essential and it's best for you to start with your rear foot positioned straight on the wakeboard.

Your lead foot should then be placed at a nine to twenty-seven degree angle when you start. Take a few seconds to determine which angle feels most comfortable to you.

As soon as you've learned the basics, you should be ready to actually get into the water and start wakeboarding.

It's a good idea to start floating with a buoyancy vest first before proceeding any further.

You should then gradually position the board perpendicular to the rope and then place your arms at the sides of your knees.

Pretty soon, you should be able to fully enjoy your wakeboarding experience and may even want to compete in the future.

Working on the
Perfect Wake

So, you're finally getting the hang of wakeboarding and you've even learned to execute jumps quite consistently.

After a few rounds, you may notice the wake getting big and crisp, perfect for some air stunts.

By this time your goal should be to get that perfect wake consistently so you can focus on practicing your big tricks and air stunts, and continue having fun, of course.

Here are a few tips to help you achieve that purpose:

1. **Line Length**

   A significant part of getting the perfect wake is using the right line length. You'll want to jump the wake just before it turns into whitewash.

   Take note that speed plays a huge role in the length of time a wake stays crisp, so you'll need to monitor this as well.

   Lengthen or shorten your line until you reach the crisp part of the wake.

2. **Speed**

The speed of your motorboat largely dictates the size of the wake and the distance it travels.

A wake generally starts to flatten as the boat speeds up and then it throws the wake further away from the boat as it becomes narrower.

As previously mentioned, your speed and line length need to complement each other.

So, when you lengthen the line, you'll have to add a bit of speed as well. Remember that consistent speed greatly enhances your ride and makes the wake a lot more stable.

3. **Trim Boat/Tabs**

How your boat sits on the water also affects the wake. It's advisable to adjust the boat's trimming once you've achieved the right line length and speed in order to really get a crisp and clean wake.

4. Seating Arrangement

The people in the boat can play a significant role in influencing the kind of wake that you get, especially if you're using a relatively small boat.

Before you start out on a ride, it's best to make sure that the people in the boat are well-balanced, particularly from one side to the other.

Once you're already in the water and you notice one of the wakes really washing out while the other stays pretty crisp, then that can be a sign that the people on your boat aren't properly balanced.

You'll be surprised at how much difference it can make to simply transfer one person to the other side of the boat.

5. Additional Ballast

Additional ballast has also become essential in trying to get the perfect wake. Many people have taken to loading their boats up with thousands of additional pounds in hopes of getting bigger wakes.

Generally, adding more weight makes the boat sit lower in the water, therefore displacing more water when it speeds up, thus resulting in a larger wake.

This is what makes people believe that adding more ballast will most probably increase the size of the wake.

Other than that, additional ballast is also expected to provide you with the flexibility of being able to move it around the boat to achieve proper side-to-side balance as well as fore-and-aft balance.

It is therefore expected to give you the ultimate wake when you ride.

By following these five tips, you should be able to look forward to bigger and better wakes.

More importantly, you should now be able to start showing off those big tricks.

Wakeboarding as Part of Your Workout Routine

Does the mere idea of spending hours at a gym every single week in an effort to stay fit exhaust you?

Going to the same location, entering the same building, and facing the same walls regularly can indeed become tedious after some time.

Running may be a more interesting way to keep in shape because it allows you to enjoy the outdoors, but not everyone finds running enjoyable.

Well, then, you may want to add wakeboarding to your workout routine.

Of course, you'll need to have the basic equipment for wakeboarding in order to be able to use it as part of your regular workout.

At the very least, you'll need to have access to a wakeboard, a motorboat, a wakeboard handle and rope, and a life vest along with some accessories of your choice.

If you already have all these, have access to them, or are planning to get involved in the sport anyway, then it can definitely offer a lot of benefits it terms of physical fitness.

It may not really be practical to consider wakeboarding as your main form of exercise primarily due to the expense it involves.

This is exactly why it's recommended only as an addition or a part of your workout regimen.

It can serve as an excellent activity to change things up a bit, enjoy the outdoors, and avoid the tediousness and boredom that can set in if you focus solely on working out at the gym.

It can be the perfect way to get away from those boring walls for a bit and forego an exhausting run from time to time.

After all, variety in exercise has been proven to help individuals stick to their fitness regimen more successfully than boring and repetitive workouts.

Wakeboarding can serve as a breath of fresh air, particularly for those who love the outdoors and water activities.

The feeling of the wind blowing against your face and the water rushing against your feet, while the mist blows all around you can indeed be exhilarating.

And this refreshing experience is just one of the many perks of including wakeboarding in your workout routine.

Another thing about wakeboarding you can be excited about is the fact that it offers a good workout for your shoulders, arms, and core muscles.

If you've ever tried wakeboarding before, even for recreational purposes, then you've most likely experienced sore muscles after the first few times of going out on the water and executing some basic movements.

If you've never tried the sport even once, then you may want to give it a try just to experience how your muscles feel afterwards, and then you'll surely understand what we're talking about.

Wakeboarding is definitely an excellent form of exercise that can help tone your muscles while expanding your muscle endurance at the same time.

Once again, we're not recommending that you replace your current workout routine with it, but it's definitely something you can use to change up your routine from time to time and have a bit more fun with your workout.

After all, getting fit and staying in shape don't have to be a chore, do they?

Keeping Your Game Up with Wakeboarding Workouts

If you love wakeboarding, but you just happen to live in a place where winters can be quite harsh, then you'll likely have to give up the sport for a few months each year unless you decide to move somewhere else every winter.

After a significant rest period, you may find that your wakeboarding skills have rusted a bit when the waters are once again ready for riding.

Furthermore, your muscles may have weakened a bit during your hibernation months, especially if the winter has been particularly long.

Fortunately, it doesn't really have to be that way.

As long as you keep working out during hibernation, then you should be able to avoid the usual season-opening problems.

Besides, you shouldn't rest from keeping fit just because you're taking a rest from wakeboarding.

Here are two exercises that can help you keep your game up even when you're not riding the wakes:

1. Drop Squats

Wakeboarding places a significant amount of stress on your legs, so it's important to strengthen your quads, hamstrings, and glutes.

For this purpose, you'll definitely benefit from drop squats. To execute drop squats, start by positioning your feet about a hip width apart.

Next, hop up while spreading your feet to shoulder width and then drop into a squat as you land.

As you reach the bottom of the squat, make sure your thighs are parallel to the ground.

As soon as you reach this position, hop up explosively as quickly as you can and then land in the starting position.

Repeat the exercise for six to ten reps.

When wakeboarding season starts, you'll surely find it easier to make those jumps.

2. Abs Wheel Workout

The sport of wakeboard demands balance, which is why keeping your core muscles strong even in the off season is very important.

This is exactly what the abs wheel exercise is all about.

To execute the exercise, grab an abs wheel machine by both of its handles and then get into a kneeling position.

Push forward slowly on the abs wheel; you're sure to feel your abs contract before you even go far into the push.

Roll as far as you can and then slowly get back to the starting position. Do three to five sets of six to twelve repetitions.

What's good about these two exercises is that they're not only great for keeping yourself fit and keeping your wakeboard game up off-season, but they're also excellent additions to your workout routine during the regular wakeboarding season.

After all, keeping yourself strong reduces your chance of getting injured when you do your wakeboarding stunts.

It'll definitely be so much easier to start the wakeboarding season if you remain consistent with your off-season workout routine.

Simply by making a little effort to maintain your strength and stamina, you can be sure to get into the water at full speed so much quicker than if took a break from working out and you can enjoy wakeboarding straight away. Have fun!

Wakeboarding: The Future?

You may have tried wakeboarding once in your life and fell in love with the sport.

The problem is that it may be too expensive for you to get into the sport and you may not really have access to a motorboat or any of the other necessary equipment and accessories.

Well, then, what we're about to tell you will definitely be good news.

There's now a new trend in wakeboarding that makes it a lot more accessible even to the average individual. You can now ride the wakes in three different ways without having to use a motorboat.

Winches, kites, and cable parks have not only made the sport significantly more affordable, but are now also offering new water terrains for you to ride.

The first alternative to wakeboarding with a motorboat is the cable park.

The sport borrowed technology from ski resort chair lifts, thus allowing you wakeboard on a mad-made lake using a rope tow that runs in a large circle around the lake.

This allowed people to enjoy wakeboarding for as little as fifty dollars per session.

These days, there are cable parks in many areas of the world and many of them have multiple lakes designed for riders of differing styles and skill levels.

The good thing about these man-made lakes is that they're designed to maintain just the right depth and are ideal for obstacles such as kickers and sliders, so you can really challenge yourself.

These are also great venues for hosting competitions, which may be why many professionals spend a lot of time honing their wakeboarding skills in cable parks.

Winches are newer and equally great alternatives for get out onto the water and riding the wakes. Winches are just about the same size as suitcases and you can purchase them for so much less than a motorboat.

Another good thing about winches is that you can easily set them up in different locations, from small ponds to docks and canals.
You can even set them up along streams, rivers, and beaches!

They can provide you with a straight line run of about five hundred feet and sometimes even more.

Many riders use winches to ride across unique water features or through rail parks.

With winches, you ride while a friend operates and you'll need just a few gallons of gas for an entire day of wakeboarding.

Perhaps the only drawback to this alternative is that it limits you to one run at a time and it runs only in a straight line.

Kites are perhaps the most exciting alternatives for wakeboarding enthusiasts like you. It has just recently been developed into a water sport of its own.

For many wakeboard enthusiasts, being pulled by a kite provides the ultimate freedom for them to ride under their own power and in any direction they choose.

It also allows them to ride through all kinds of water, even ones that are just a few inches deep, which will never be possible with a boat.

Although a bit more complicated than other alternatives, the rewards of wakeboarding with a kite are definitely unequalled in the sport.

Whatever alternative you choose, though, wakeboarding has definitely become a sport that not only the rich can enjoy year-round.